BEI GRIN MACHT SICH IHR WISSEN BEZAHLT

AF149918

- Wir veröffentlichen Ihre Hausarbeit, Bachelor- und Masterarbeit

- Ihr eigenes eBook und Buch - weltweit in allen wichtigen Shops

- Verdienen Sie an jedem Verkauf

Jetzt bei www.GRIN.com hochladen und kostenlos publizieren

Victoria Schwer

Thoughts on Ishmeal Beah's Novel "A Long Way Gone, Memoirs of a Boy Soldier"

An essay

GRIN Verlag

Bibliografische Information der Deutschen Nationalbibliothek:

Die Deutsche Bibliothek verzeichnet diese Publikation in der Deutschen National-
bibliografie; detaillierte bibliografische Daten sind im Internet über http://dnb.d-
nb.de/ abrufbar.

Impressum:

Copyright © 2012 GRIN Verlag GmbH
Druck und Bindung: Books on Demand GmbH, Norderstedt Germany
ISBN: 978-3-656-59471-0

Dieses Buch bei GRIN:

http://www.grin.com/de/e-book/268437/thoughts-on-ishmeal-beah-s-novel-a-long-
way-gone-memoirs-of-a-boy-soldier

GRIN - Your knowledge has value

Der GRIN Verlag publiziert seit 1998 wissenschaftliche Arbeiten von Studenten, Hochschullehrern und anderen Akademikern als eBook und gedrucktes Buch. Die Verlagswebsite www.grin.com ist die ideale Plattform zur Veröffentlichung von Hausarbeiten, Abschlussarbeiten, wissenschaftlichen Aufsätzen, Dissertationen und Fachbüchern.

Besuchen Sie uns im Internet:

http://www.grin.com/

http://www.facebook.com/grincom

http://www.twitter.com/grin_com

Victoria Schwer

English 2

13 November 2012

Ishmael Beah and his courageous life

A Long Way Gone, Memoirs of a Boy Soldier is a memoir written by Ishmeal Beah. The book

was published in 2007 and it´s about a young boy, Ishmeal, who lost his family and became

an unwilling young boy soldier during the civil war in Sierra Leone. He has been turned into a

killing machine capable of horrible violence.

This book is based on his true story, experienced by himself. It´s gives the reader such a good

impression and understanding how it is to have a live in the army and how courageous

Ishmeal is.

Especially in some special parts of the story, the reader gets an absolutely great impression

of how his life was. Really good parts to get a better understanding of his life are his thinking

times. He is sharing his whole mind with the reader and they are definitely pretty

interesting.

The first really good part is, when he is in the rehabilitation center of UNICEF. Like a couple of times, he is thinking about his life and what happened.

"Little did I know that surviving the war that I was in, or any other kind of war, was not a matter of feeling trained or brave. These were just things that made me feel I was immune from death" (Ishmael 159).

This quote shows the reader exactly what he is thinking and how he is feeling of his whole life. He is definitely not thinking that he was brave and courageous. He is pretty much sure that this war was just a really bad time in his life and he didn't deal with that great, he dealt just like everyone who has to be in this situation, but the reader gets a completely another impression. Not everybody is that strong enough to survive and then trying to get a normal life back, that's definitely the hardest part. His village has been attacked and so he lost his whole family, that's really hard for a twelve-year-old boy. From this point on, he has to take care of himself and trying to survive without money, a home, food and everything. Then the army becomes his "family" and he gets brainwashed into believing that each rebel death may avenge his own family's slaughter. He is turning into a killing machine. All these facts have made his life so hard and complicated. And I think definitely that he is the bravest and most courageous boy ever even when he isn't thinking that. Especially, when you are strong enough and have the desire to get back to a normal life, then you are courageous. Not everyone is strong enough and can keep the wish for a better life, but Ishmael got it! And that's the reason because I can say he is brave!

Another really good part of the story where you can see how courageous Ishmael is, is when he is getting moved from the rehabilitation center to his uncle´s family in a city called Freetown. Of course he is really happy to have one part of his family left but he is also very worried about getting a part of his new family.

"I was afraid that I might look ungrateful to my uncle, who didn´t have to take me in, if I distanced myself from the family unit" (Ishmael 179)

This quote shows us very clearly that he is so grateful and happy that he can live in his uncle´s family. They are the only people who he is related to and who are left. He really wants to change his life and his attitude, and makes the best out of his situation. To get the possibility of living that new life it is absolutely important that he is getting along with his relatives, that´s the most important process. If that´s not going work then he will probably fall back to his old life and can never get over his bad experiences, and that´s the big issue he is worried about. With other people he is really distanced and afraid to talk to them, especially when they ask about his past. However he needs to talk a lot and become a part of his new family. I believe he is definitely on the right way. His attitude is really good and I guess he is really strong enough to overcome this.

A last really good part of the story is, when he is in New York. That´s the time, where he gets the chance to tell the whole entire world his own story.

"I was confident that nothing could get any worse that it had been, and that thought made me smile a lot" (Ishmael 202)

Actually, this quote shows the reader a lot of what he is thinking from his life and about his attitude now. He is so convinced that it can´t get even worse than his past was, and I think maybe he´s right. I guess it´s true. His life was so hard that it´s almost impossible that something bad happened again though I really like his way of thinking. He is so much more positive now and just trying to make the best out of the new life. He shouldn´t be mad and upset about what happened, he should just be positive, because it´s definitely going to be better and now he has the best premises to make it better.

Finally, I can definitely say that this story is one of the best I have ever read. It really touched my heart. While I was reading it, I was getting more and more mad about the world. It makes me so sad that there are not enough people and things to help all these soldier kids. In my opinion, it's an awesome book, and I got such a good impression how the life is going on there. I absolutely promote this book and everybody should read it. I think there should be so many more stories about this type of life. Because of this book, the kids get more attention from the whole world and so they have a bigger chance to get a better life.

The most important thing that I learned out of this book is:

Every single person in the world should help to improve this situation because not only a few kids are concerned with that horrible life. No! Unfortunately there are so much more…